FASHIONIZE 2
illustration will rule the world

happybooks

illustration:
TOSHIFUMI TANABU

FASHIONIZE 2 selected by Delicatessen

Happy Books, Italy ISBN 978-88-86416-69-6

Concept:
cristiana valentini & gabriele fantuzzi
www.delicatessen.it

Art direction:
gabriele fantuzzi@delicatessen

Distribution:
www.happybookstore.com
happy@happybooks.it

Website:
www.mondofragile.com
info@mondofragile.com

COVER
SOPHIE GRIOTTO

BACK
HYPNOTEIS

THIS PAGE
GRAND PEOPLE

FASHIONIZE 2 © 2007 First published in Italy by Happy Books srl

Thanks to all involved in and around FASHIONIZE 2 book, way too many to mention, but you all know who you are...

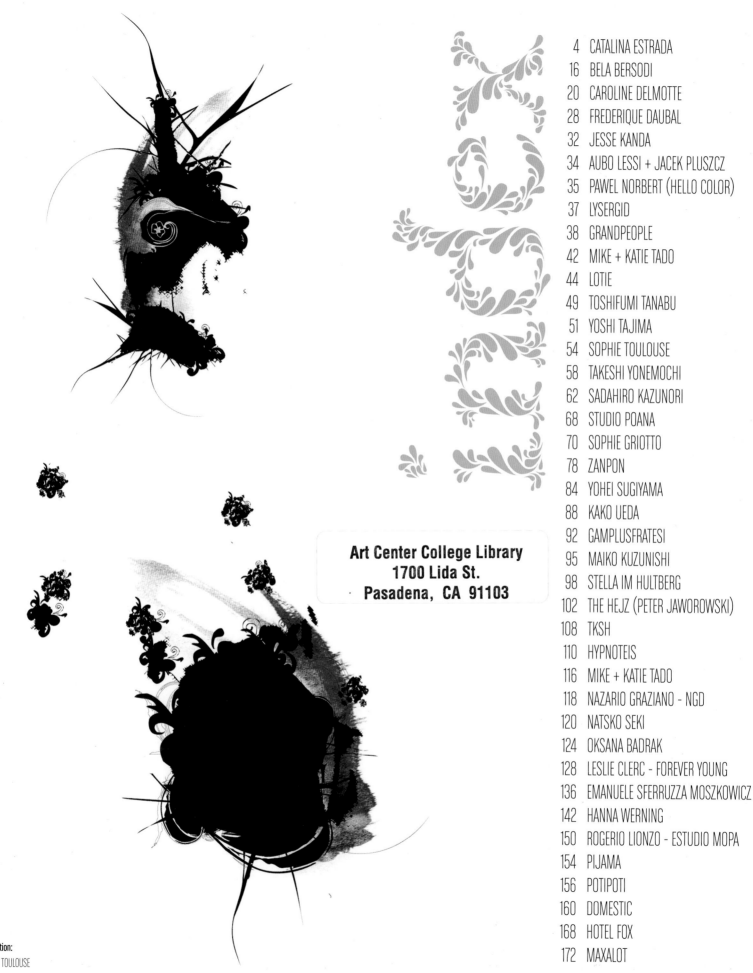

illustration:

SOPHIE TOULOUSE

ANUNCIAÇÃO, 2007 Art director: ANA CHRISTINA DA ROCHA LIMA - Designer: MARIA ELVIRA CROSARA Photo: ROGEIRO MESQUITA

CATALINA ESTRADA

FOR

ANUNCIAÇÃO

ANUNCIAÇÃO, 2007 Art director: ANA CHRISTINA DA ROCHA LIMA – Designer: MARIA ELVIRA CROSARA Photo: ROGEIRO MESQUITA

ANUNCIAÇÃO, 2007 Art director: ANA CHRISTINA DA ROCHA LIMA - Designer: MARIA ELVIRA CROSARA Photo: ROGEIRO MESQUITA

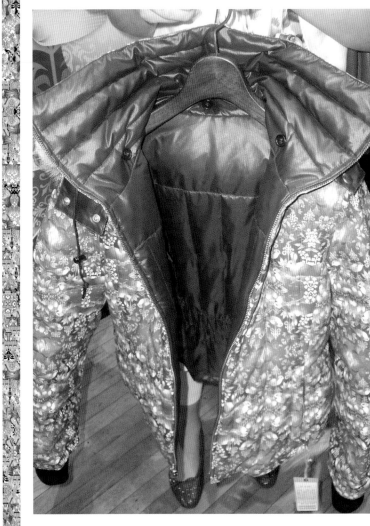

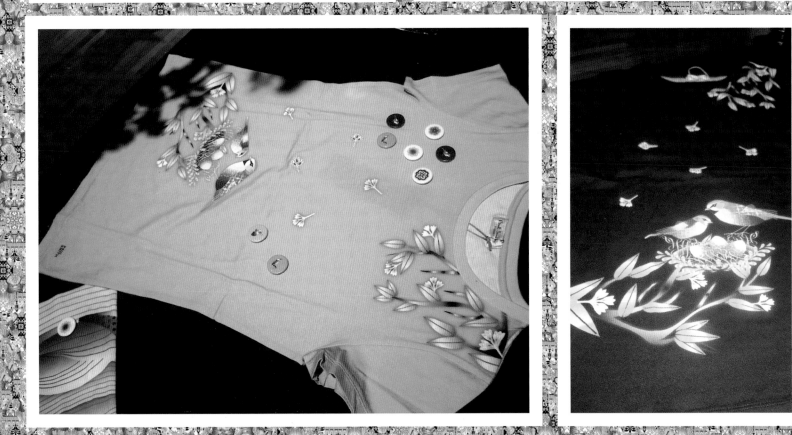

"SHOEZOO" KID'S WEAR #22 - Photographer: © Bela Borsodi - Fashion Editor: Catrin Hansmerten - Printing: Junsik Shin @ Solo

"SHOEZOO" KID'S WEAR #22 - Photographer: © Bela Borsodi - Fashion Editor: Catrin Hansmerten - Printing: Junsik Shin @ Solo

STILE magazine italy - Sylist: irma birka

STILE magazine italy - Sylist: irma birka

VALEUR   NUTRTVE

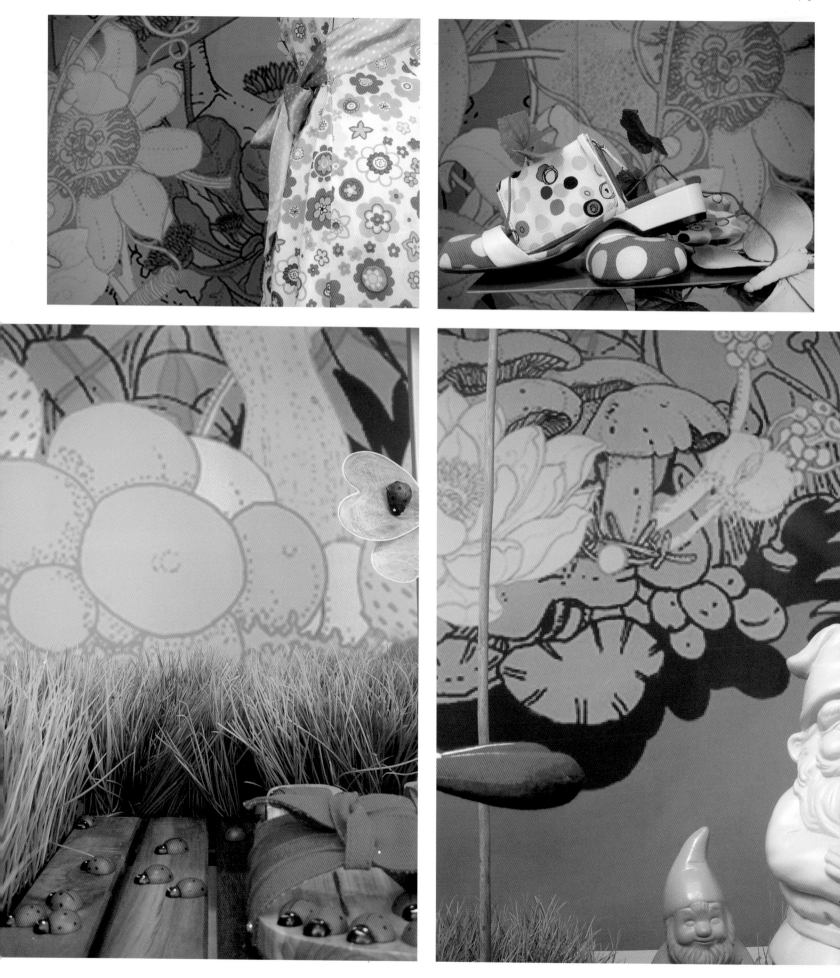

d a z e d a n d c o n f u s e d j a p a n c o n g r a t u l a t i o n s o n t h e 3 r d a n n i v e r s a r y .

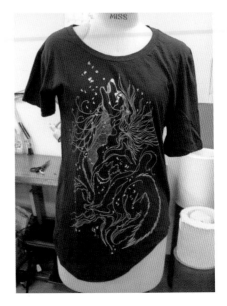

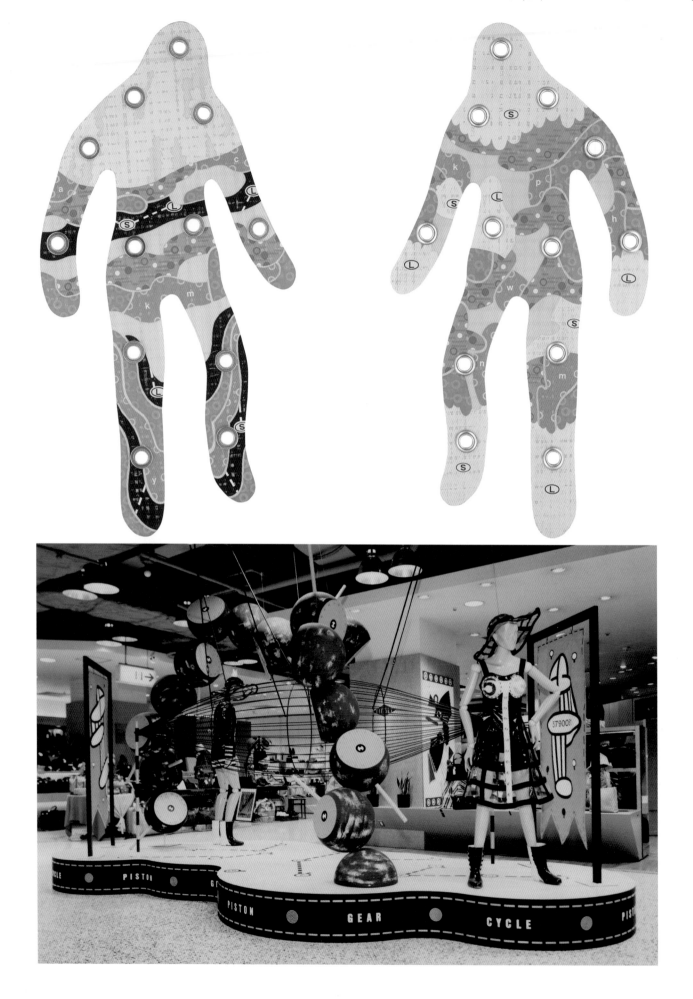

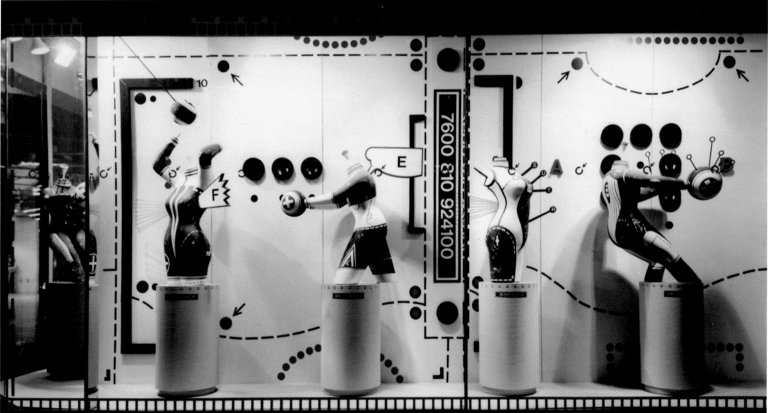

JART.INC
SKATEBOARDS

FRANCK
BARATTIERO
ROBBER & SWINDLE EXPERT
SINCE 1963

JART.INC
SKATEBOARDS

EERO ANTTILA
KICKFLIP'S WISE WIZARD

JART.INC
SKATEBOARDS

ORLANDO
ACOSTA
MYSTICAL VOODOO SINCE 1922

JART.INC
SKATEBOARDS

MATHIEU DUPUY
ROUGH DOGGY STYLE
SINCE 1895

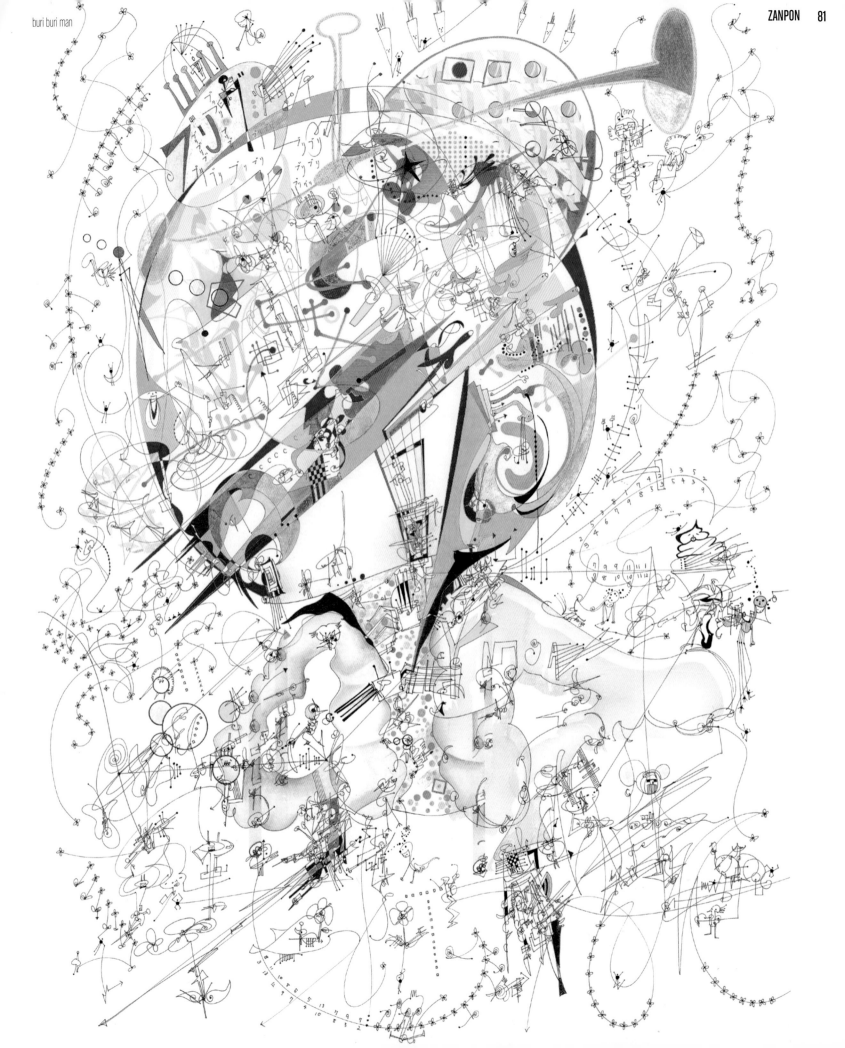

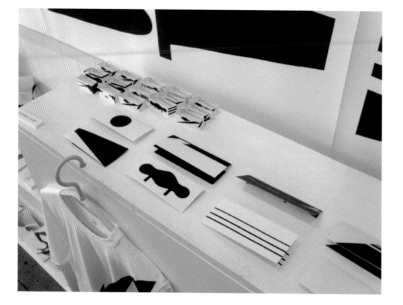

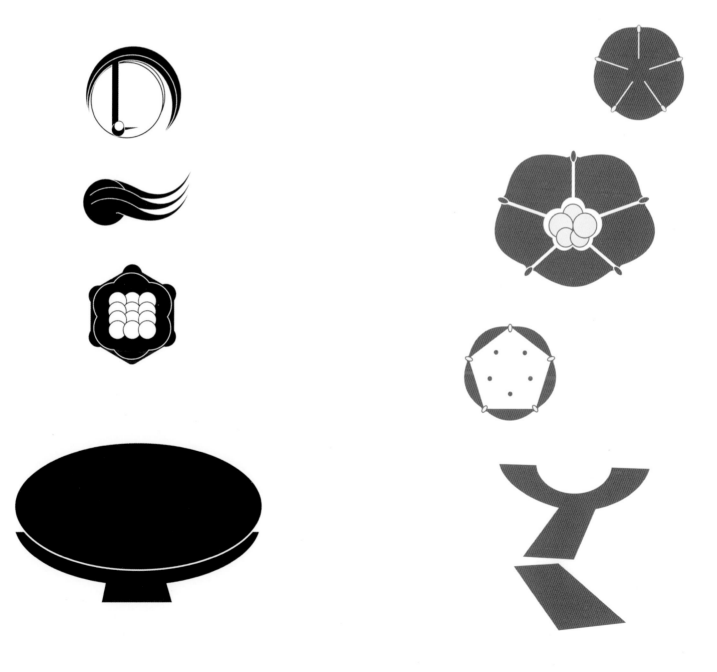

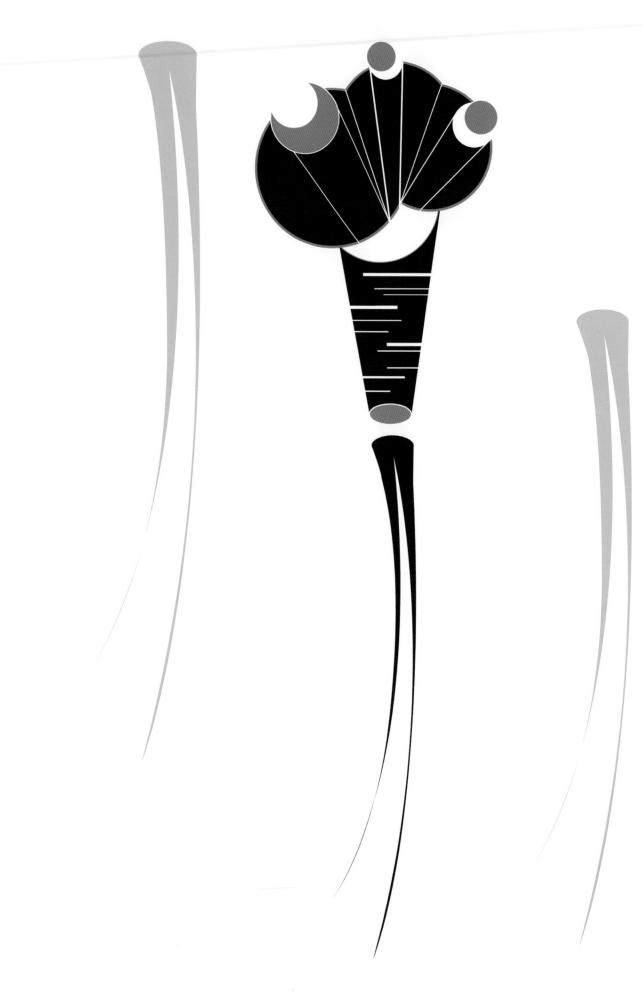

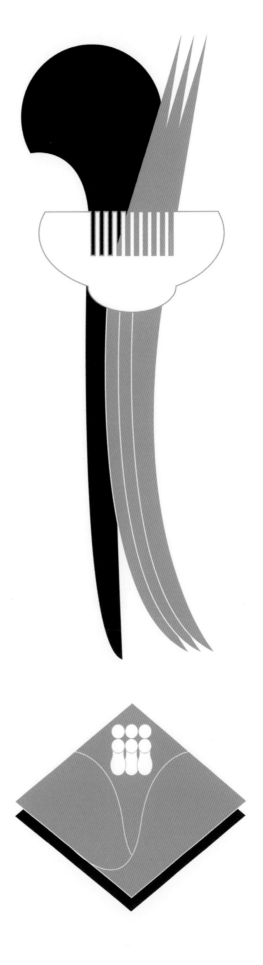

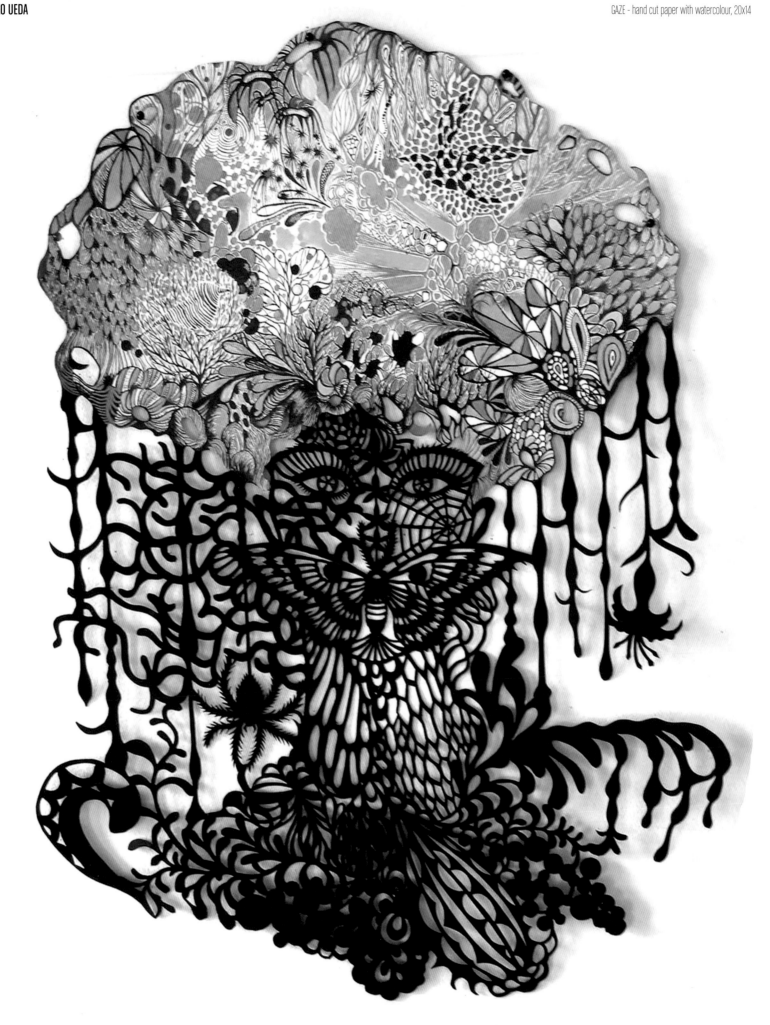

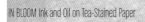
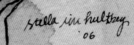

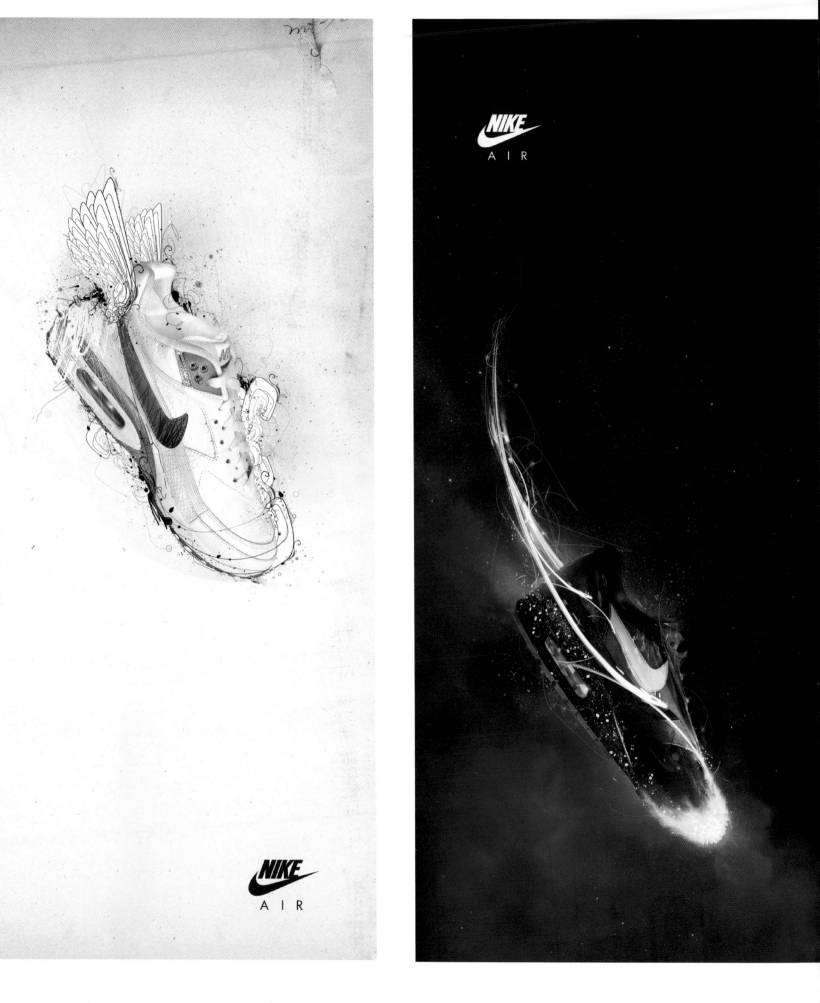

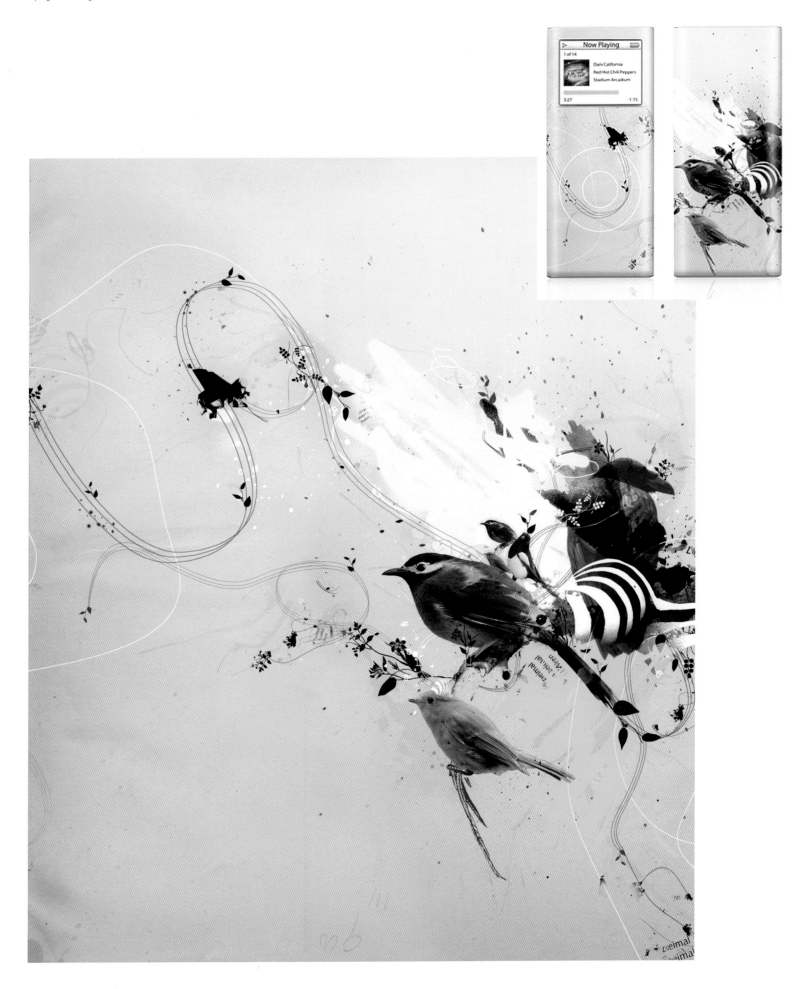

Nokia L'Amour
Embrace the emotions.

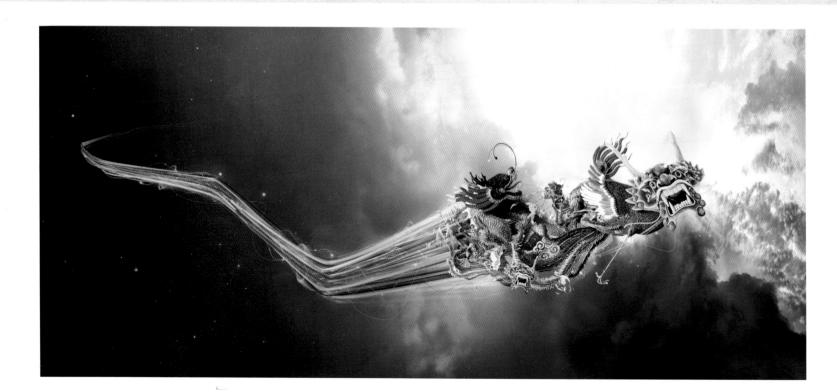

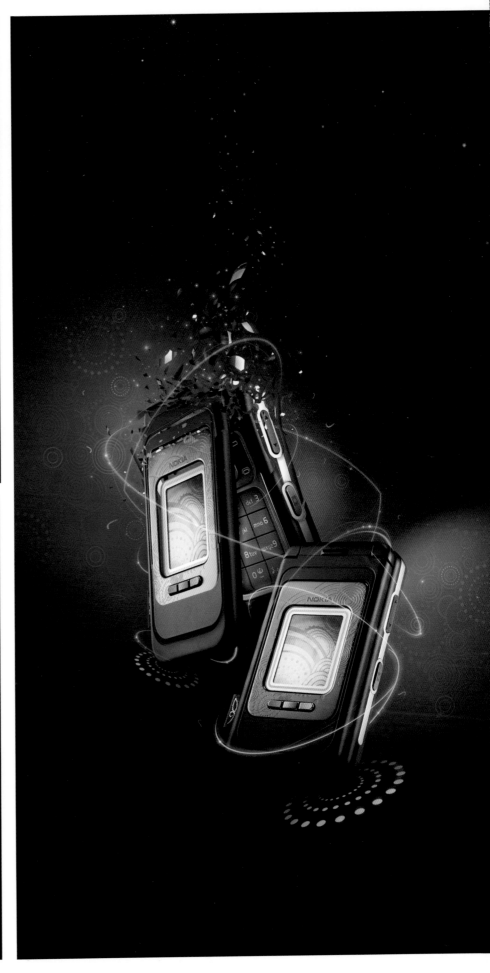

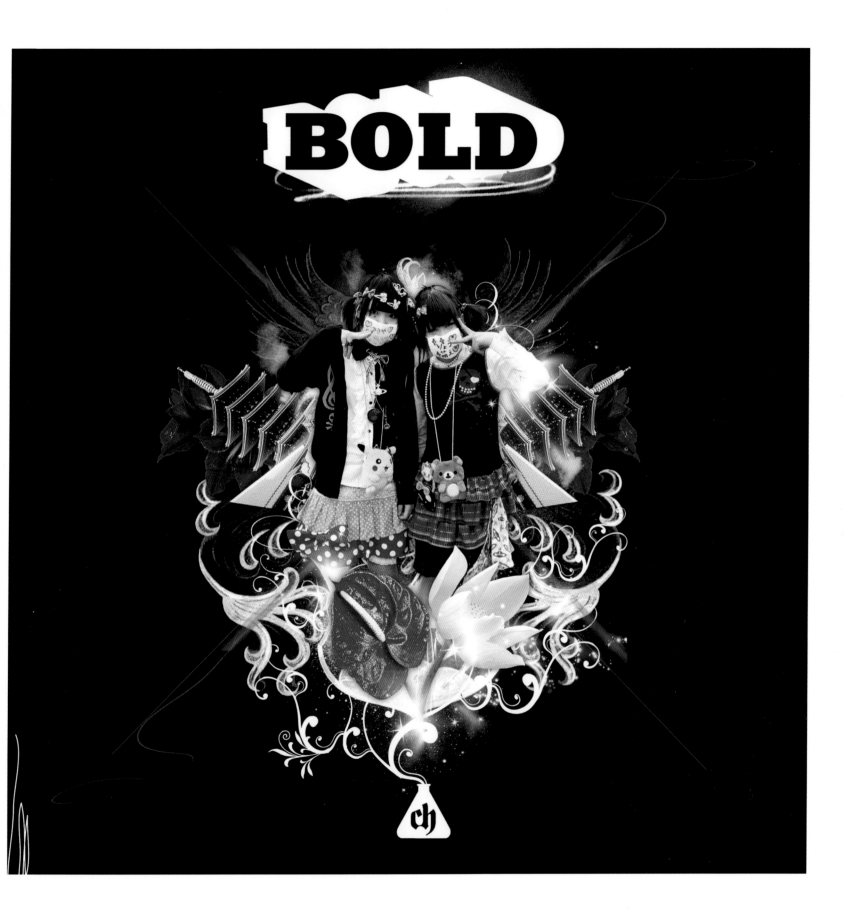

ABOVE > nice flat , Toshin ni sumu magazine BELOW > < not buying it, Elle Decoration (U.K.)

NATSKO SEKI   121

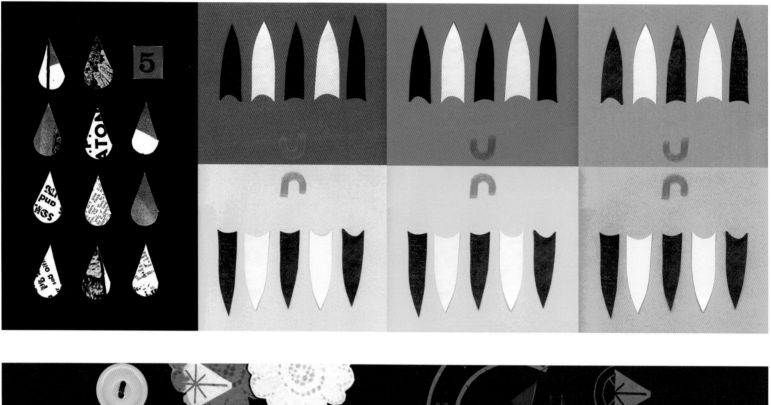

ABOVE left > music , Paper Sky magazine (Japan) right > Guitar, personal work BELOW left > piano, personal work right > books, Paper Sky magazine (Japan)

NATSKO SEKI 123

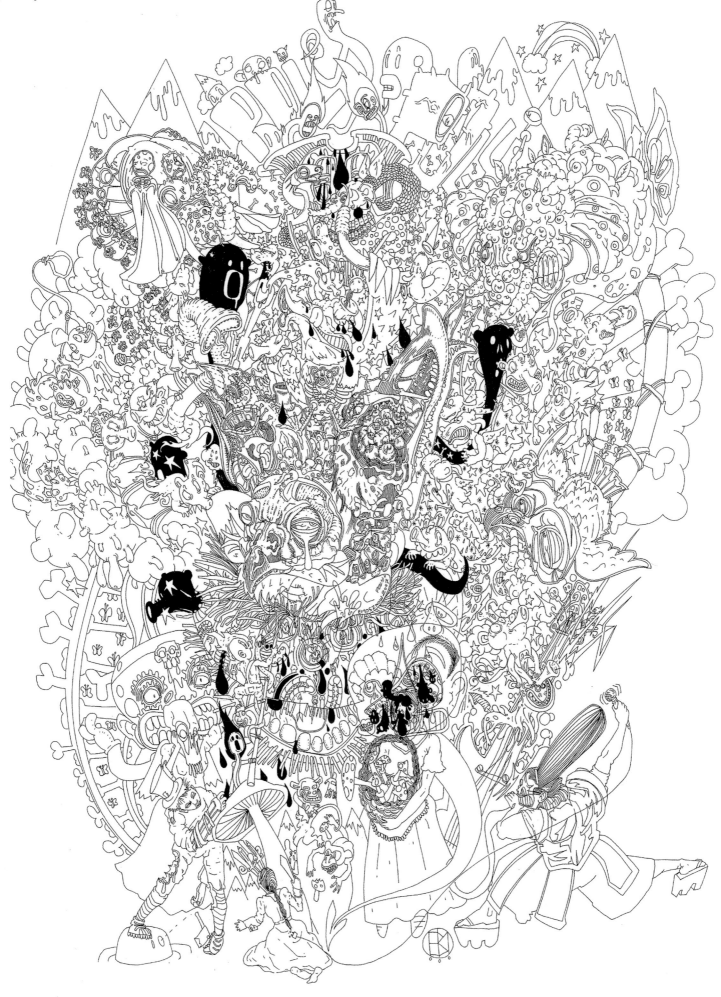

ABOVE > DJURTRÄDGÅRD & FJÄDERLÖV, textile prints - Client: Borås Cotton, Sweden BELOW > ALICE & SENS, Textile print for cushion and bags - Client: Alice & Sens

ROGERIO LIONZO / ESTUDIO MOPA 143

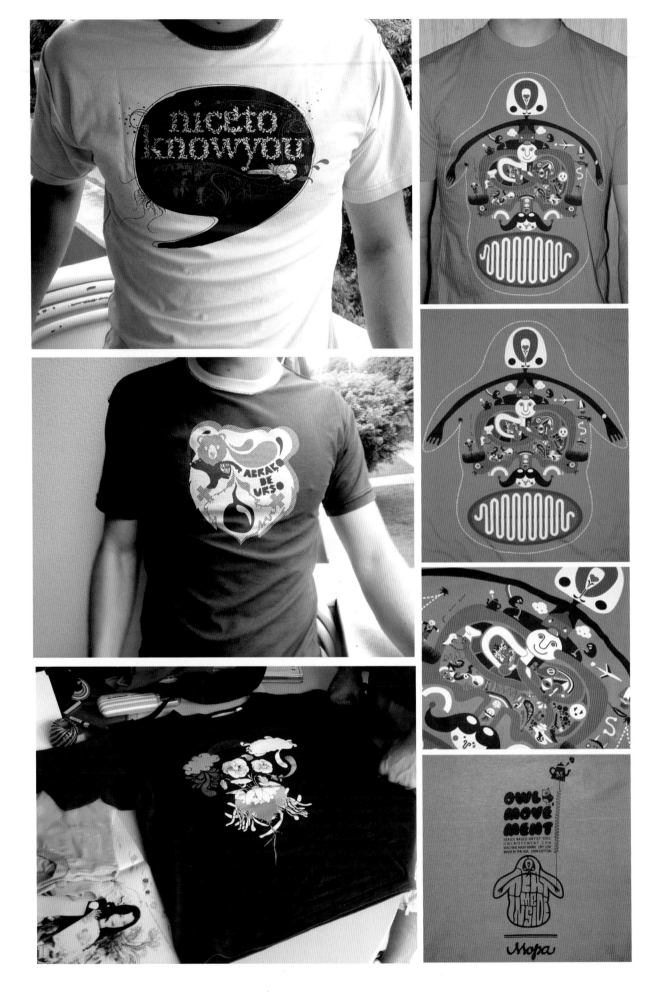

ABCDEFGHI abcdefghijklmn
JKLMNOPQR opqrstuvwxyz
STUVWXYZ 1234567890

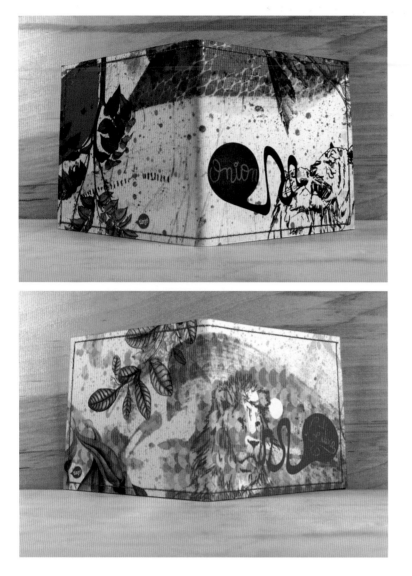

154 PIJAMA

soft cases for PC laptop. Iphone, vinyl, digital camera ...

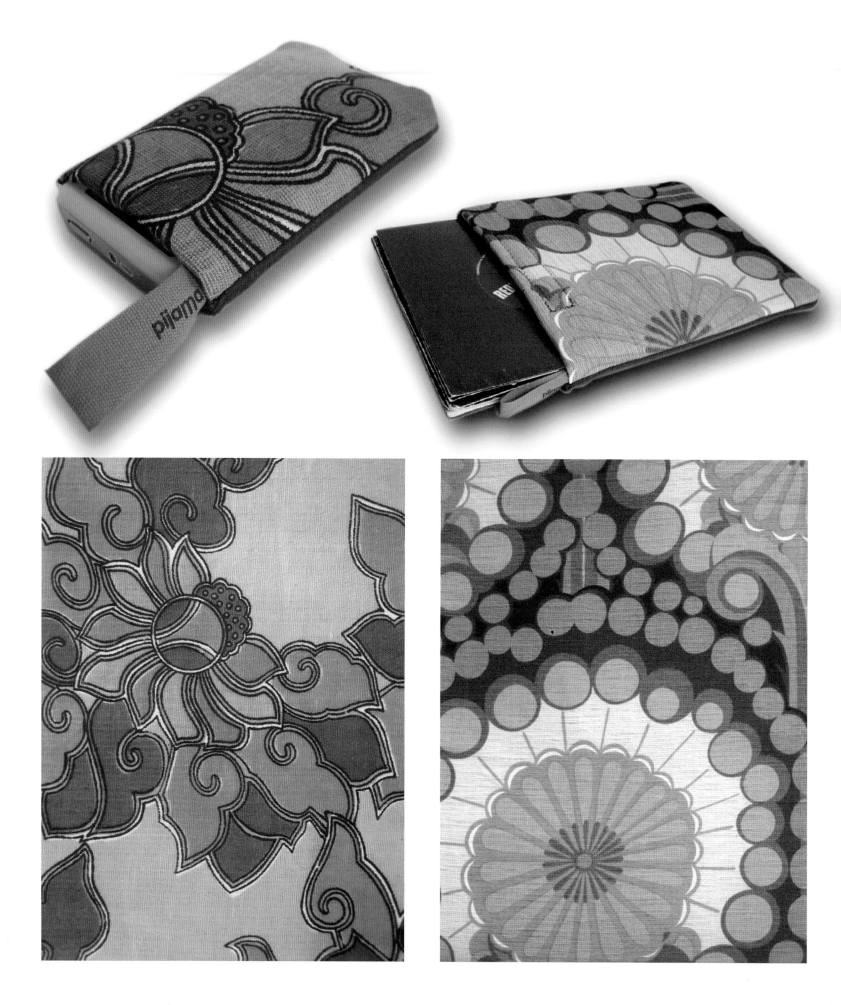

soft cases for PC laptop. Iphone, vinyl, digital camera ...

PIJAMA 155

"Fábula" S/S 07 Photos models: RIAN HELLER Models: Amanda und Tim Make Up & Hair: Annete Kamont Sun Glasses: Linea De by potipoti, General Optica Shoes: KTW for potipoti

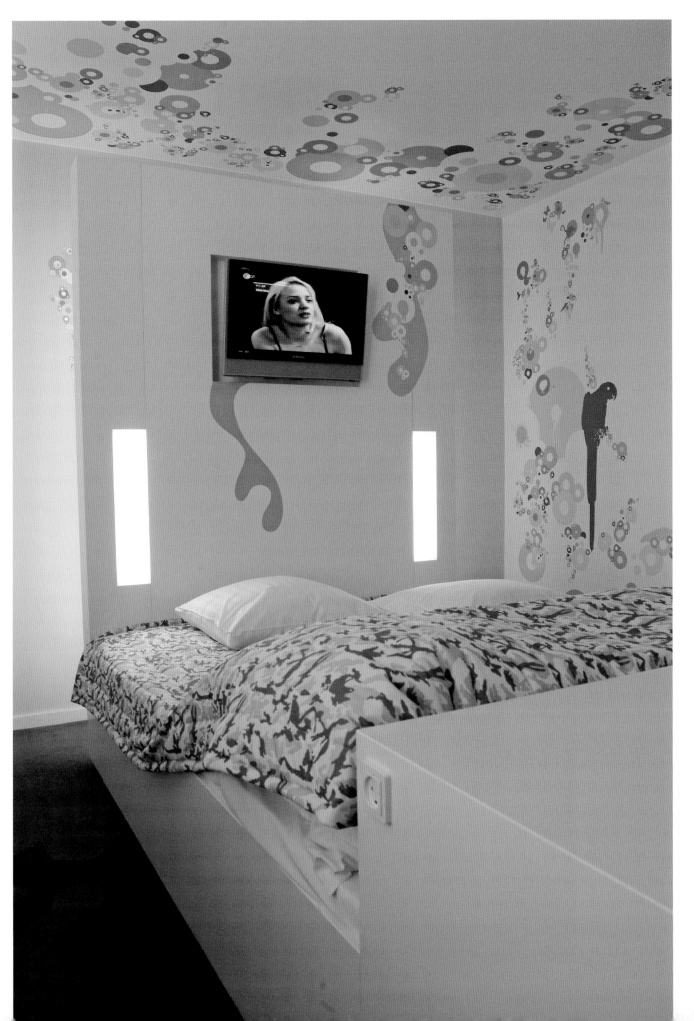

The Basilisk

Cerberus

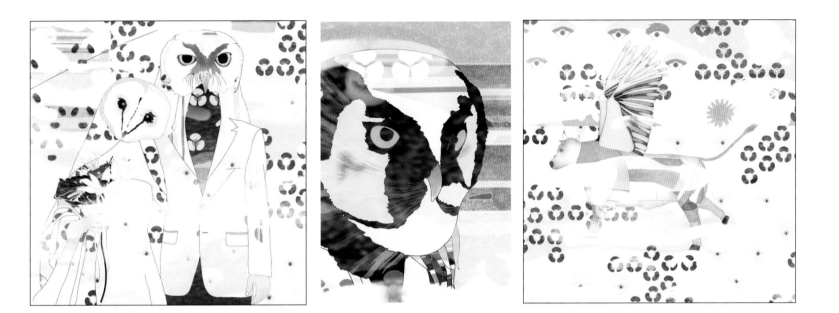

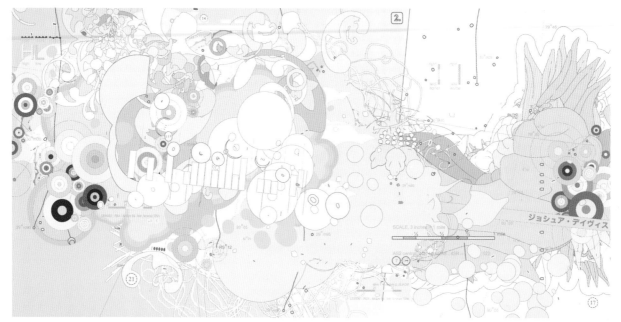

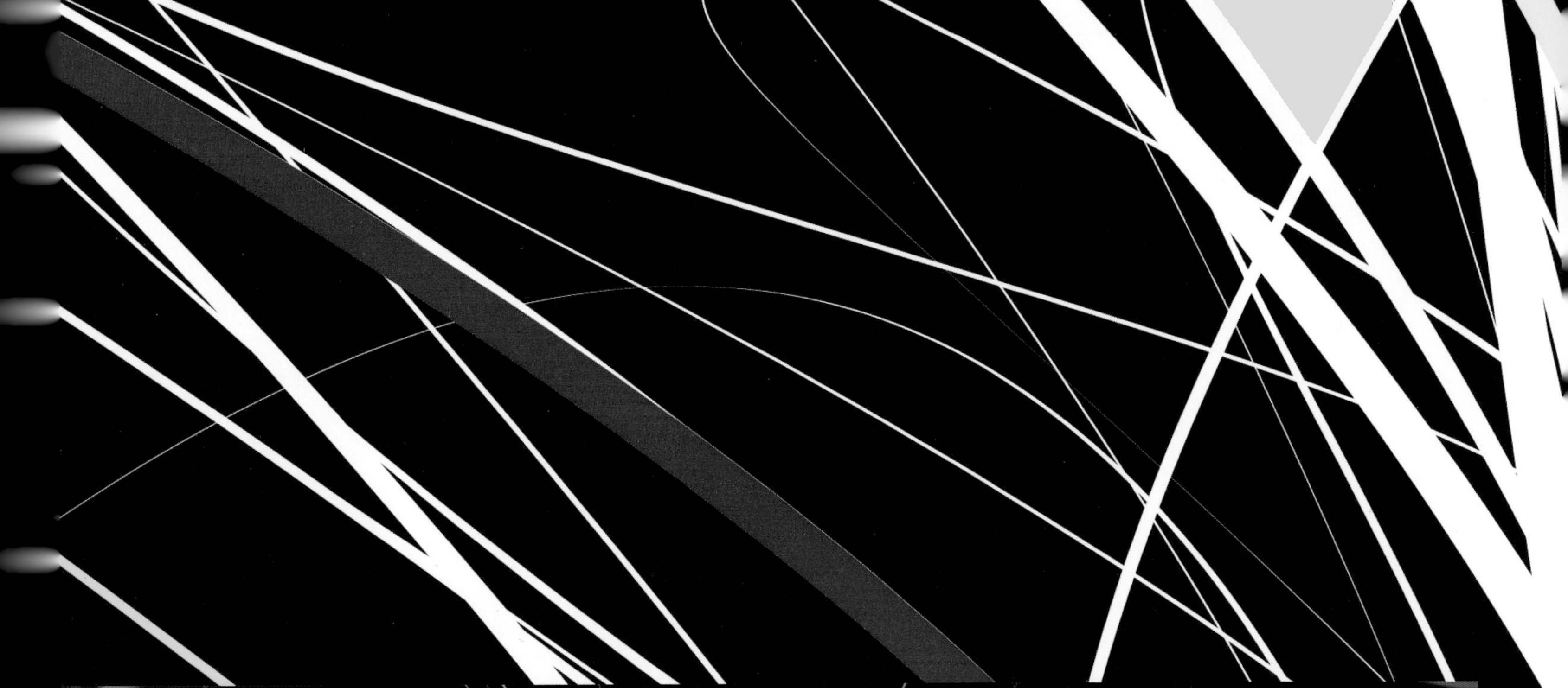

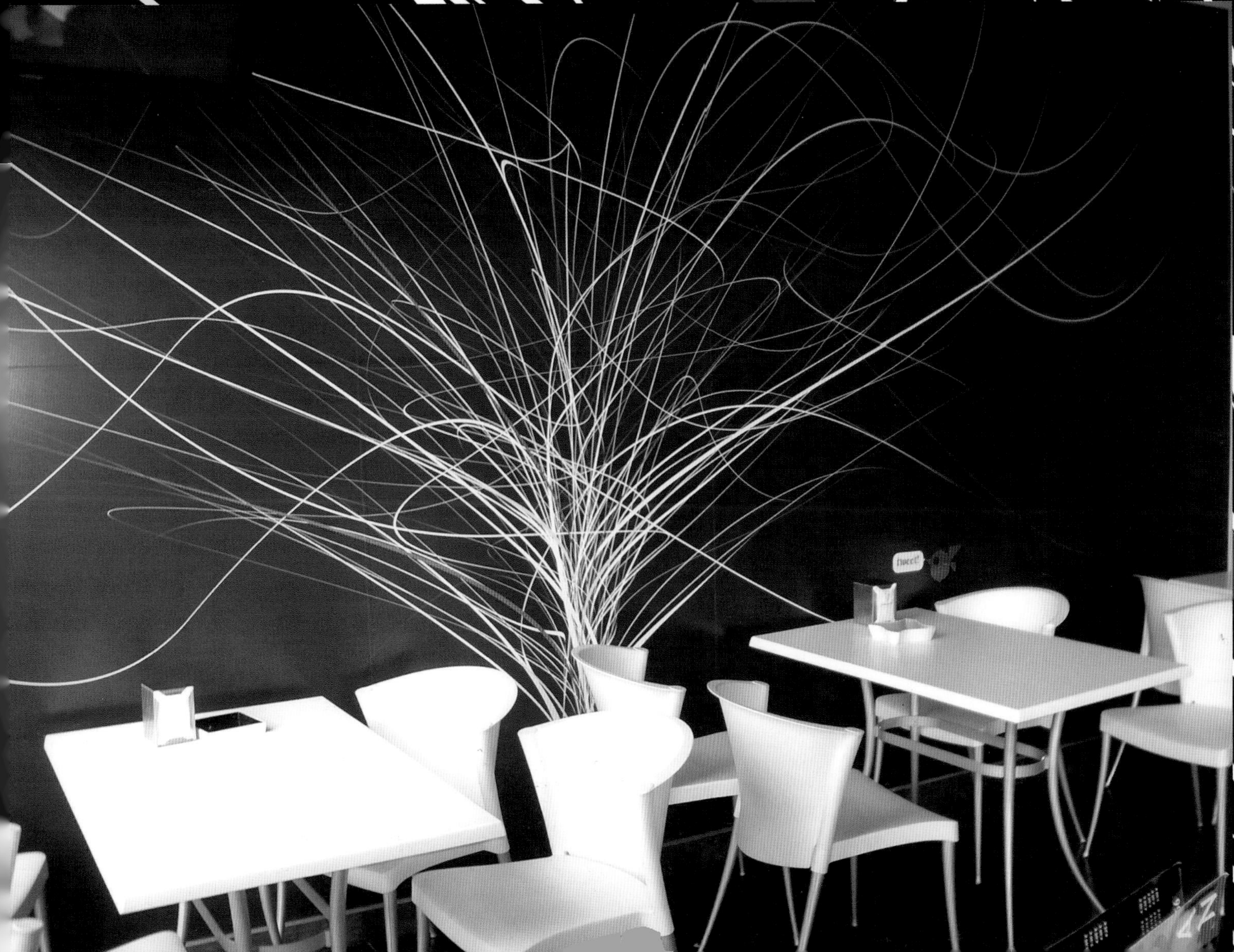
tweet!

92-94

GAMPLUSFRATESI STUDIO

overgaden oven vandet 8

christianshavn

1415 copenhagen

denmark

tlf. denmark: +45 51900117

tlf. italy: +39 3475606607

mail: gamplusfratesi@hotmail.com

www.gamplusfratesi.com

95-97

MAIKO KUZUNISHI

908 w. 89th st.

kansas city, mo 64114 usa

(816) 333-6690

www.decoylab.com

maiko@decoylab.com

98-101

STELLA IM HULTBERG

www.stellaimhultberg.com

contact@stellaimhultberg.com

102-107

PETER JAWOROWSKI

THE HEEJZ

ul. zelazna 38 m 57

15-298 bialystok

poland

www.hejz.com

peter@hejz.com

108-109

TKSH

www.stillontherun.new.fr

stillontherun@gmail.com

110-115

HYPNOTEIS

TEIS ALBERS

antwerpenstraat 46

5224 te 's-hertogenbosch

the netherlands

www.hypnoteis.nl

info@hypnoteis.nl

118-119

NAZARIO GRAZIANO | NGD

www.ngdesign.it

me@ngdesign.it

120-123

NATSKO SEKI

studio26, 26 rosebery avenue, london,

ec1r 4sx, u.k.

www.natsko.com

mail@natsko.com

124-127

OKSANA BADRAK

oksana@badrak.com

www.badrak.com

128-135

LESLIE CLERC

FOREVER YOUNG

75 rue pigalle 75009 paris / france

tél: +339 52 80 11 82 / +336 60 40 0304

www.forever-young.fr

www.myspace.fr/leslieclerc

136-141

EMANUELE SFERRUZZA

MOSZKOWICZ

emoszkow@gmail.com

www.chewinfloordrobe.blogspot.com

142-149

HANNA WERNING

Upplandsgatan 50

SE-113 28 Stockholm Sweden

+46 (0)70 236 57 25

www.byhanna.com

hanna@byhanna.com

150-153

ROGERIO LIONZO

shin qi 07 conjunto 15 casa 18

lago norte brasília - df - brazil

rogerio@estudiomopa.com

www.estudiomopa.com

www.lionzo.com

154-155

PIJAMA

www.pijama.it

info@pijama.it

156-159

POTIPOTI

silvia salvador and nando cornejo

choriner str. 50

10435 berlin

 germany

tel.: +49.30.20339804

mob.: +49.176.24247174

email: info@potipoti.com

wwww. potipoti.com

160-167

DOMESTIC

19 bis, rue jean-baptiste sémanaz

93310 le pré saint gervais

france

tèl : + 33 (1) 48 45 94 60

fax : + 33 (1) 48 45 94 79

www.domestic.fr

stephane@domestic.fr

168-171

HOTEL FOX

BRØCHNER HOTELS A/S

Nørre Søgade 11

DK-1370 Copenhagen K

Direct tel: +45 3395 7715

Adm. fax: +45 3395 7701

www.brochner-hotels.dk

172-182

MAXALOT

C / Palma de Sant Just, 9(a-b)

08002 Barcelona

Spain

tel +34933101066

www.maxalot.com

lot@maxalot.com

delicatessen

cristiana valentini + gabriele fantuzzi

italy

www.delicatessen.it

info@delica.it

Delicatessen is represented in Europe (except UK) by

ILLUSTRISSIMO

Michel Lagarde - michel@illustrissimo.com

www.illustrissimo.com

Delicatessen is represented in America+UK+Japan by

KATE LARKWORTHY ARTIST REPRESENTATION, LTD

182 Norfolk Street #3 New York 10002

www.larkworthy.com

kate@larkworthy.com